T0145197

The Kyoto Mirror Pond Poems

Dwight Cavanagh

To order additional copies of this book, contact:
Xlibris
844-714-8691
www.Xlibris.com
Orders@Xlibris.com

ISBN: Softcover   978-1-6698-0547-2
            EBook   978-1-6698-0546-5

Print information available on the last page

Rev. date: 02/22/2022

Dedication

To Lynnie, Catie, Joseph, Page
and Brooke with love.
And profound thanks to Jennifer Roemer for
her help in preparing this collection of poetry.

Table of Contents

Ugi River Fireflies

Hotaru nō hikari: Firefly Glow

Kami[1] of dead samurai[2]
Swarm as fireflies in Ugi's sky
Winking in June's[3] summer night,
Poised in the reeds for sudden flight;
Sparks cast from the FORGE OF BEING[4],
Screeing[5] o'er the BRIDGE OF SEEING[6],
To the HIGHER PLANES OF MEANING[7];
Hobbled by hard karmic[8] choices;
Seduced by MAYA's[9] SIREN [10]VOICES;
Soaring again HOME TO THE LIGHT.[11],[12]

---

1   Kami: Spirits of the dead
2   Warriors of the Path of Bushido: "Death is lighter than a feather; duty is heavier than a mountain."
3   Ugi River in Yamashita Prefecture is famous for its ancient bridge and marsh fireflies.
4   The Well of Souls
5   From the Old Norse, "moving;" Old High German "going"
6   Meditation; The path between planes of existence
7   Ascending planes of existence until Nirvana
8   Karma: Ribbons derived from interference with the spiritual or physical development of other souls.
9   Maya: The Hindu Sanskrit Goddess of Illusion
10 The Lorelei: who call sailors to destruction
11 Rebirth on the wheel of Samsara in Buddhism
12 See also Richard Bach's The Bridge Across Forever (1984) for additional context.

Für Rolfe – Ich hatt' einen Kameraden

Es is Zeit zu gehen.
Nicht zu kämpfen
Ohne Ende
Als Betragen

ORDINAL ONE

SERVER'S CANTO
Kannon's Bells

Kannon's Bells in sadness ring
For the pathos of all sentient things;
That are and were and
Again will sing!

ORDINAL ONE

SERVER'S CANTO
As Long As....
For Longfellow
(CHORUS)

As long as hearts have reasons,
As long as rivers flow;
As long a minds have passions,
As long as flowers grow;
As long as years have seasons,
As long as winters snow;
As long as loves have treasons,
Sly secrets none can know.

ORDINAL TWO

ARTISAN'S CANTO
Choices

All is chosen;
Choice is king
No fate is frozen
'til Kannon's Bells ring.

ORDINAL TWO

ARTISAN'S CANTO
Play Up
(CHORUS)

A poem without a rhyme;
A painting without a frame;
Fear running out of time;
Terror without a name.
Cadence without a number;
Boasting without shame;
Sleep without slumber
PLAY UP! PLAY UP THE GAME.

ORDINAL THREE

WARRIOR'S CANTO
Zeit Zu Gehen (Time to Go)

The journey of the years is done.
The exit bell has rung.
Lady Kannon's song is sung.
Es ist Zeit zu gehen.
It's time to go.
Across the river SADNESS
Over the bridge REGRET,
Through the slough of MADNESS
To Lethean sleep FORGET.
Let be. It's time to go.
Time's swift waters flow,
Don't be last or slow;
Or pose for shallow show.
Es ist Zeit zu gehen
NICHT ZU KÄMPFEN;
It's time to go.
A new PLAY starts again
Where fresh choices grow
That's all we know:
Es ist Zeit zu gehen.
It's time to go;
Und weiter so?

ORDINAL THREE

WARRIOR'S CANTO
Takeda Shingen[1]
(wind, forest, fire, mountain)
(CHORUS)

The wind is swift
Silent forest sleeps deep;
From the fire bold flames leap.
Above them all the mountain stands
Immovable, strong above the lands

---

1   *Takeda Shingen (1521-1573) was Lord (daimyo) of Kai Province and perhaps the greatest military general in feudal Japan. He was called the "tiger of Kai" and his battle standard displayed: "Wind, Forest, Fire, Mountain: One should attack one's foes as swift as the wind, as quiet as the forest, as aggressive as fire, as strong as the mountain."*

NEUTRAL FOUR

SCHOLAR'S CANTO
C'est Tout II

The autumn leaves fall like tears
Blowing in the wind;
To mark the passage of the years
For what has been
Or might have been.
And will be again.
THE PLAY goes ever up and on;
On birth's stage with first breath began.
And we must journey as we can.
And trust THE PLAY.
And trust life's plan.

NEUTRAL FOUR

SCHOLAR'S CANTO
Kyoyochi: The Mirror Pond
(CHORUS)

Is a single word a poem?
Is a single note a song?
That rings late the chimes of meaning
Written on the mirror pond of being
With karma's iron pen of fate.

CARDINAL FIVE

SAGE'S CANTO
Ryoanji: Place of peaceful dragons

They say the
nesting mallards keep
the pond where peaceful dragons[1] sleep;
Hard by the Mirror
Pond of Being[2]
With the inner eye of seeing,
In dark dreaming deep.

---

[1] Ryo (dragon) angi (peaceful place)

[2] The Ryoyochi or Mirror Pond (13th century) is the pond adjacent to the Zen monastery of Ryoanji in Kyoto, which has the classic "raked whitestone" garden. The pond mirrors the Golden Pavilion Kinkakuji, purchased in 1397 by the Ashikaga Shogun Yoshimitsu for his retirement.

CARDINAL FIVE

SAGE'S CANTO
(CHORUS)
KOKORO

Time the beating
heart of being
Through the long years
of illusion seeing
In the mirror courts
of meaning
To awaken from
deep dreaming.

CARDINAL SIX

PRIEST'S CANTO
Tokugawa Iyesu

The servant came and
told the three:
The nightingale will not sing!
Nobunaga[1] cried, "kill the bird"
Hideyoshi[2] cried, "quite absurd"
Their advice was strong and wrong;
Iyesu[3] waited for the song.

---

1   Oda Nobunaga (1534-1582), military dictator and unifier of feudal Japan.
2   Hideyoshi Toyotomi (1537-1598), sage, poet, samurai and polymath of the Momoyama period of feudal Japan (1573-1615), Hideyoshi's successful rival for rule was Iyesu Tokugawa.
3   1543-1616, First Tokugawa Shogun of Japan

CARDINAL SIX

PRIEST'S CANTO
The President's Grand Cocktail Party
(CHORUS)

I had THE dream again
last night;
And despite all my fright,
Could not make it fade 'til morning's light.
And, as each face slipped away,
I saw none left but an
empty hotel hall,
With a long and aching loss,
In a moment gone astray.

CARDINAL SEVEN

KING'S CANTO
Der Fliegende Holländer[1]

As fools we cry when
seen too late
We are but pilgrims on the
sea of fate.
A timeless sea without a shore.
And only the journey evermore.

---

1 *Richard Wagner's operatic masterpiece, The Flying Dutchman. The Dutchman's ship will never port.*

CARDINAL SEVEN

KING'S CANTO
The Play Without an End
(CHORUS)

A bird without a song;
A leaf lost from a tree;
A ship without a course;
On a shoreless angry sea;
Night without a candle;
Evening without a star;
Sin without contrition
With a judgment none can mar;
Autumn without falling leaves,
Swirling in the wind.
Call bells ringing in the eaves
To THE PLAY that has no end.

Dwight Cavanagh, M.D., Ph.D., matriculated at MIT (Boston, MA) and went on to complete his A.B. and M.D. degrees at Johns Hopkins University (Baltimore, MD), and Ph.D. at Harvard University (Cambridge, MA). During a career spanning more than 50 years as an eye surgeon, visual scientist, and educator, Dr. Cavanagh served on the medical faculties of Harvard, Johns Hopkins, Emory University (Atlanta, GA), Georgetown University (Washington, D.C.), and UT Southwestern Medical Center (Dallas, TX). He retired from UT Southwestern in 2020 and enjoys his Professor Emeritus status. Dr. Cavanagh currently lives with his wife Lynn Gantt Cavanagh in Dallas and has had a lifelong interest in colonial history, genealogy, poetry, philosophy, Japanese culture, and Zen.

Publication of The Kyoto Mirror Pond Poems completes the Kyoto Poems trilogy of The Tao Poems (2006) and The Kannon Poems (2011).

List of Illustrations